The Marital Bed:

A Lil' Lookie at the Nookie

A Book of Love Stories, Discoveries,
Advice, Challenges and Activities
to Add Spice to Your Sex Life

By Sandy Buchanan-Sumter

The Marital Bed: A Lil' Lookie at the Nookie

Copyright © 2018 by SBS GBABIE Enterprises

Printed in the United States of America

First Printing, 2018

ISBN: **978-0-692-17792-1**

SBS GBABIE Enterprises
Laurel, Maryland
www.sbsgbabieenterprises.com

Reviews

"The Marital Bed" is every couples desired odyssey through love's passionate passage. You'll find no other book that captures your pleasure, your panties, and your praise all in the same enclosed space. After reading, you'll barely put it down before finding yourself reenacting Sandy's tips and tricks of the marital bed. As a newly married couple, this has not only enlightened us on the importance of romance, but also ignited our bedroom in a major way! *Joshua and Anastasia Parker, Newlyweds*

Whether you're newlyweds or have some years behind your marriage, Sandy offers some excellent advice from a God-centered perspective. It's honest and funny – definitely a good read. *D. Reed, Writer/Author*

I have always been comfortable talking about sex but uncomfortable when it came to talking specifics about what I like and don't like. Even though I've been married for 5 years, I'm still shy when it comes to telling my husband what I need. But reading this book has encouraged me to be more vocal not only in what I need but also in asking him how I can please him more. *Brooke N. Hawkins, Co-President, Mocha Moms, Inc., Southern P.G. County Chapter, Author/Editor/Blogger*

This book is a much-needed accompaniment and bedside guide for couples to read. It presents some serious need-to-know information in a light-hearted and fun way. It is a great read, and I encourage all to pick up a copy now. Singles looking to get married can benefit, too, as they'll be ahead of the game. *Donna E. Tillery, Entrepreneur/Editor*

My Prayer

Marriage is honorable among all, and the bed undefiled; but fornicators and adulterers God will judge. ***Hebrews 13:4 NKJV***

Oh Lord, my God, how excellent is Thy Name in all the earth! I bless Your Name, Father God. You are so worthy. Thank you for your Son, Jesus, who died just for me! Lord, I'm just so grateful and thankful for my life and all it encompasses knowing that all things work together for my good! I've weathered many storms, ups, downs, trials and tribulations triumphantly only because of You. I'm thankful for You, Lord, for being there for me when no one else was and for accepting me with all my mess. Thank You for loving me with a love that is endless, boundless, and unconditional. I love You today and forevermore.

Forgive me, Father, for those things I've done that were not pleasing to you. Lord, have mercy on me for the spirit of procrastination that kept me from working on this book that you deposited in my spirit in 2012. Thank you for being my Almighty Daddy who knows all and sees all and for extending Your hand of correction and convicting my spirit when I have displeased You. Yet You are so kind and merciful toward me despite all my mess – Your grace and mercy continues to abound in my life, and I'm grateful.

Thank you, Lord, for the gifts, talents, and visions you've given me. May they be used to edify Your Kingdom. I pray that each and every reader be blessed, enlightened, and strengthened by what You have given me to share. Use my hands, my mind, and yes, even my wit, Lord God, for Your Glory.

Lord, I pray for those struggling in their marriages and those still discovering themselves and each other in marriage. My prayer is that marriages be bound together with Your Love where they seek intimacy with You, both individually and collectively, and that their relationship would be further strengthened through the intimacy they share in their relating to one another. Lord, You said in Your Word that marriage is honorable among all and the bed undefiled, so, Lord, open the minds and hearts of married couples to love one another purely, more freely, and without shame so as to enhance their marital bond.

My life is rich because of You and the people you have carefully placed in my life for a time such as this! Thank you, Lord, for the love and support of Your people, who have given me guidance, love, and encouragement while moving forward with this work. Bless them all, Lord!

Thank you, Father, for when I need clarity and guidance, You are my Counselor; when I feel overwhelmed and hopeless, you are my Hope; when I'm in need, Lord God, you are my Provider; when everything seems chaotic in this crazy world, you are my Peace; in setback after setback and distractions, you are my Promise Keeper and Encourager; when my heart is heavy, Lord, you are my Comforter and my Burden Bearer. Lord, You are the Author and Finisher of my faith. Thank you for being my Light as I walk this path to fulfill the vision You have set before me, and I will do so in the spirit of Your Love. When I am weary, You are my Strength and My Song. Without You, I am nothing. Use me, Oh God, and I will be ever so careful to give you all the glory, honor, and praise. I remain grateful and thankful in ALL THINGS! Amen and Hallelujah!

Dedication

I dedicate this book to my husband James, my sister and best friend Pam, my mom Delma, and my son James who have all gone on to glory. I also dedicate this book to my sons, Xavier and Cameron, who had to witness all the public displays of affection between James and I. NO APOLOGIES!

It's been said that the three most prevalent reasons that marriages fail are sex, money, and communication. It also has been said that the number one reason is sex. However, sex is also the most glorifying aspect of marriage. God created sex for two basic purposes—procreation and pleasure. So why is there so much taboo surrounding this very beautiful activity. What does God say about sex? Let's go to the Bible.

In the book of the Bible, Song of Solomon, we see how two people respond to each other in the celebration that sex really is. The book starts out in Chapter 1, verse 2, we see these words written "Let him kiss me with the kisses of his mouth" (NKJV). This is the beginning of a love song. Kissing is a very powerful and erotic tool, and usually the beginning of the act of lovemaking. And intercourse is not the only aspect of lovemaking. But let's look deeper. In chapter 3: verse 1 we read, "By night on my bed I sought the one I love." (NKJV) We must seek each other. It doesn't just happen. We must be intentional.

Let's continue. We must speak to one another. Words are very powerful. Let's look at how Solomon used words to heighten our pleasure; to set the table if you will. In chapter 4, verse 3 we hear "your lips are like a strand of scarlet, and your mouth is lovely." (NKJV) In verse 5 we hear, "your breasts are like two fawns, Twins of a gazelle." (NKJV) Just look at the imagery. Can you imagine hearing those words spoken while lying on your marriage bed? Shall we go further? In verse 16b, we see "Let my beloved come to his garden and eat its pleasant fruits." (NKJV) The word garden in this context refers to her body. He used his mouth and tongue on her body; and she used hers on his body.

Why did I spend so much time quoting the Bible? The marriage bed is ordained by God as being "undefiled." Nothing that happens between a husband and wife that is consensual can be bad. There is nothing that goes on that can be considered dirty or evil or defiling. God knew what he was doing! He set everything up for our pleasure. Romans 8:28 says "All things work together for good for those who love the Lord and are the called according to His purpose." (NKJV)

As you read "THE MARITAL BED", please read it with an open mind. Please don't be negative about what you read. If you open your mind, this book will invigorate your sex life, and breathe new life into your marriage. What you read is NOT theory. Everything in this book is "tried and true;" proven to work activities. If you put these techniques into practice, your sex life and your marriage will go to new heights of pleasure and intimacy.

So, read the book, and GO FOR IT!
Deacon William G. Gentry, Jr.
Chief Financial Officer, First Baptist Church of Glenarden
Leader/Speaker/Mentor of Men

Acknowledgements

I want to shout out all my cheerleaders, family, friends, and all encouragers who prayed for me and believed in me and my work, I'm commissioned by God to do this. He said it, I believe it, so I'm pressing on! Pray for me and be watchful, because there's more to come! Know that if God has given you a vision, He has already given you what you need to fulfill it, whether it's a book, business, ministry, or whatever, KNOW that HE is not just working it out, but that HE has already WORKED it out. Diligently work your life's purpose and await the manifestation! It's already done! Don't toil over the minute details and get stuck like I did. There are people out there that need you, your gifts, and talents. Trust God! Walk into your destiny! Know that God will put the right people and other resources in your path, like He did with me. He literally dropped folks and opportunities in my lap! God really shows off, yall. He is everything. Boom. Mic drop!

Well, if you know me and know my story, you can guess who I dedicate this book to! If you don't know, well, you'll learn something about me (and him) today. Though he has gone on to Glory to be with our Almighty Daddy, I dedicate this book to my husband, James (whom I called "Dad" after we had children), aka Sump (as most of his friends and family called him) aka Big Daddy (as most of MY friends called him, lol). He was a kind and gentle man with a heart of gold. He truly was my biggest supporter in life, my best friend and partner, my technical assistant when I was performing psalmist activities, and my lover in every way possible (He TURNT up in the bedroom, too, yall!). He was a great husband and a fantastic father. He helped me become the person I am today. I'm thankful and forever grateful for the time God allowed me to have with him. He's one of my many angels now, and I know he's smiling with me right now. Love you always, Dad!

I dedicate this book Pam, who also has gone on to Glory. I have to acknowledge her, as she was my eldest sister and my best friend in the world. As a little girl, I would beg to sleep in her bed when I was frightened (and she'd give in) and as an adult, I would pack a bag and go to her place to hang with her for the weekend. She was Nanny to my children and their Godmother, too. She was less likely to be freaky with her man and if she were still here, she'd give me the side eye about my book and say, "Umph. Girl, you are so crazy."

Continue to rest in paradise, my beloved sister. I miss you so much!

I also dedicate this book to my Mommy, Delma, who I know is smiling down on me from Heaven! She was my HEART! My mother, in her kind and gentle way, always was open to communicate about matters of the heart and anything else, for that matter, and answered any questions I had. No conversation was off limits and no subject taboo. She was my example for showing passion and love toward my husband though she was always meek and humble. Simply put, she was PRECIOUS to me. Thank you, Mommy, for being that example for me. I carry you with me always.

A shout out to some of my biggest cheerleaders in life: Donna Tillery, my true roadie, right-hand person, sister, and friend, who willingly serves in whatever capacity I ask; William "George" Gentry, my big brother and Dad figure who always provides advice and keeps me on track; his wife, Belynda, whose spirit is as sweet as a Georgia peach, who inspires me and leads by example of what a Godly woman, wife, and mother should be; Lakisha Davis-Small, who is a self-motivated visionary who continues to cheer me on and give me opportunities to shine my light; Joshua and Anastasia Parker, who I've claimed as brother and sister, a power couple who are true examples of how God blesses when you do things HIS way; Tawawn Lowe, for the PUSH, the recommendations, resources, and tough love when I was being timid and laxed; and finally, Dr. Shauna Moore Reynolds and Linda Lane, for listening, guiding, supporting and being God's confirmation mouthpieces! Thank you all for the prayers, conversations, and simply for believing in me. I love you all to the moon and beyond!

Finally, I dedicate this book to my amazing sons. James Allen, though you closed your eyes forever on December 2, 2017, know that you've always been a part of me, and I will forever hold you dearly in my heart. To Xavy and Cam, I know you were scarred by watching Mommy and Daddy smooch and other PDA's, but I thank God that you witnessed a healthy, loving relationship between husband and wife. You never stifled the "yucks" and "eeeswwwss" lol. If only the walls could talk. Love you guys... you continue to be the apples of Mommy's eye!

A Message from the Author

Then he said to them, "Go your way, eat the fat, drink the sweet, and send portions to those for whom nothing is prepared; for this day is holy to our Lord. Do not sorrow, for the joy of the Lord is your strength." Nehemiah 8:10 NKJV

The joy of the Lord is my strength! What would I do without Him? I realize, absolutely nothing. I love the Word of God and its revelations. I know you do, too. So you'll see it throughout this work. Some scriptures relate to the particular chapter, some don't. No matter what or where it's placed, the Word is always good.

It's 2012. God deposited in my spirit a book that would help relationships between husbands and wives. "Where do I start, Lord? I'm not licensed to counsel. Who's going to listen to little ol' me? There are so many public figures with 'marriage' books on the market. There are so many roads I can go down. Do I focus on communication, finances, trust, or something else?"

I was definitely confused and self-doubting. I realize that was the enemy infiltrating my mind to keep me from moving forward. The devil is a liar and the truth ain't in him!

So one day as I was driving up 295 from DC after a long day of work, I heard God clearly say "The Marital Bed" and I immediately got excited. Then, I got nervous.

"God, how will people receive this? I have no credentials. I'm not a sex therapist. How do I share what I know so that people 'get it' and are not offended and, most importantly, that You are well pleased?" Well, God said, "just be you and you'll touch the right people who are meant to receive the message. You have hands-on experience (no pun intended) so just teach people how you and James loved each other."

Thank you, God! He reminded me that I may not have the credentials to write anything clinical, authoritative, or preachy, but am I an authority figure on my life experiences, what I've observed in other married couples, and things that have worked in connecting with my lover. Herein, I'm simply sharing me, my life, my understanding, my thoughts, and my experiences in a way that only I can and in a way that My Almighty Daddy and my Big Daddy Hubby James are proud of. As Christians in the sanctity of our marital covenant, we are FREE and not bound by stereotypes of what people think we should be – we don't have to be prudish when loving on our spouse, praise be to God Almighty! I'm thankful for that because I like to get "freaky" with my man (don't gasp... we'll talk about "freaky" in the book... lol).

This book is for all the married couples who are looking for a funny read together (separately works, too) and some insight into having more fun in the bedroom (or wherever you want to spice things up — kitchen, tub, the closet for a quickie? lol). Because I love to tell stories, I share some stories and scenarios in this book. I hope and pray you will be challenged in your sex life to communicate more and work toward a little more spice in that area. Think outside the box. Be creative. Have fun with one another.

We all know there are challenges in every union but nothing is too hard for God! -- not finances, communication, and definitely not "lovin." This book is birthed from fond memories of fun times with my husband James; life experiences and witnessing the good and the bad in marriages throughout the years; roundtable discussions and conversations with friends and family on marital issues; and, finally, my desire to see relationships flourish.

Who knows, maybe this book will make the divorce rate will go down! It's frustrating for me to see the flippant attitudes toward marriage and divorce. Folks, God can change your relationship if you seek and trust HIM! (Ooops, let me step down off my soap box.) Again, nookie isn't everything and it's not going to solve all marital issues... but it's a GOOD thing and an active, spicy sex life dang sure can't hurt! Lol.

Intimacy in a relationship is very important and comes in many forms; it's not just the physical climax (though that is YUMMY, lol). What I can promise you is that, if you open your mind, allow the creative juices to flow, and have some fun with your bae then you can and will experience a rebirth of or add a little spice to your physical relationship. If you allow it, you will be intrigued and stimulated to try something new or different. With great hope, you'll laugh and be inspired to be freer to new experiences in your love life! I won't lay out everything for you but I will encourage you, though, to put some effort into pleasing and getting to know your partner more intimately.

So, let's do this! Are you ready to have fun and be inspired? Let's take this journey together. Indulge me as I tell stories and paint mental pictures. Let it encourage you, challenge you, and bless your union! I'm not speaking clinically – this is just real talk from my perspective, observations, and experiences. If you think you'll be offended then put the book down now. Know that the intimacy we explore in this book first begins with living holy – knowing and loving God and what He would approve of in a loving, committed marriage. Living holy is your ultimate goal. In doing this, you will please your spouse! I will speak about "happy" and "happiness" in the book. Understand that I use it in the context of living a holy Christ-centered life. There's nothing immoral or corrupt about loving on your spouse. Do what's pleasing and acceptable to both parties involved with Christ being the center of the relationship. I encourage you to take some notes as you read through it – use it as a reference and by all means, have fun with each other!

"If I speak in the tongues of men or of angels, but do not have love, I am only a resounding gong or a clanging cymbal. If I have the gift of prophecy and can fathom all mysteries and all knowledge, and if I have a faith that can move mountains, but do not have love, I am nothing. If I give all I possess to the poor and give over my body to hardship that I may boast, but do not have love, I gain nothing.

Love is patient, love is kind. It does not envy, it does not boast, it is not proud. It does not dishonor others, it is not self-seeking, it is not easily angered, it keeps no record of wrongs. Love does not delight in evil but rejoices with the truth. It always protects, always trusts, always hopes, always perseveres.

Love never fails. But where there are prophecies, they will cease; where there are tongues, they will be stilled; where there is knowledge, it will pass away. For we know in part and we prophesy in part, but when completeness comes, what is in part disappears. When I was a child, I talked like a child, I thought like a child, I reasoned like a child. When I became a man, I put the ways of childhood behind me. For now we see only a reflection as in a mirror; then we shall see face to face. Now I know in part; then I shall know fully, even as I am fully known.

And now these three remain: faith, hope and love. But the greatest of these is love." 1st Corinthians 13:4-13 (NIV)

Table of Contents

"For this reason a man shall leave his father and mother and be joined to his wife, and the two shall be come one flesh. This is a great mystery, but I speak concerning Christ and the church. Nevertheless let each one of you in particular so love his own wife as himself, and let the wife see that she respects her husband." Ephesians 5:31 – 33 (NKJV)

Chapter 1 – Frisky, Fun, Freedom

Chapter 2 – The Prerequisite to Funning:

"Mama Says Clean It Up!"

Chapter 3 – Set the Dinner Table

Chapter 4 – Mind-Loving: Foreplay Before Foreplay

Chapter 5 – Foreplay:

Licky-Licky Before the Sticky-Sticky

Chapter 6 – Get Your Freak On

Chapter 7 – The Love Story

Chapter 8 – A Little Dab'll Do Ya

Chapter 9 – Trips, Toys, Timbs, and Tasty Treats

Chapter 10 – Protecting the Love Nest

Epilogue (or something like that) – Let's Wrap It Up

Chapter 1

Frisky, Fun, Freedom

You will show me the path of life; in Your presence is fullness of joy; at Your right hand are pleasures forevermore. Psalm 16:11 (NKJV)

There is a time for serious matters and then there's time for fun! Loving time is fun time. Something my mother said to me has stuck with me like Gorilla glue. "If it's not fun and doesn't feel good, don't do it." My mother had nine children, so I know she was having fun and getting her freak on. She was an authority figure on how to have fun in the bedroom. I thank God for my mother and the freedom I had to discuss such things with her.

Even being in a wheelchair didn't stop her from enjoying her husband. Yes, they still made love as elders, y'all! I learned so much from my Mommy about keeping the connection and spice alive! I used to tease her about the "velveteen rub" when she got married in her later years. If you don't know what that is, just think about leaving the false teeth IN THE JAR beside the bed! *Hahahaha!* I digress!

When I think about the romps I had with my husband, boy did we have fun! From quickies, to planned scenarios, to role playing, to putting on Timberlands for traction (lol), and the list goes on. The sanctity of the marital covenant is a wonderfully freeing gift from God for you to enjoy one another in Him. Accept it. Appreciate it. Praise God for it!

So, in my attempt to provide clarity, throughout this book, I'll define things based on my thoughts of what they are in a loving committed marriage relationship. So for starters, let's define NOOKIE! Warning!... Don't look it up in the dictionary or even Google it. (That's going to make you look it up, right? Lol). Anyway, I found that it is described as a vulgar term. Very interesting, and I'd say strange. I still can't understand why it's described that way. The root of the word NOOKIE is perhaps from the word, "nook" which simply means "a corner or recess, especially one offering seclusion or security." How the word NOOKIE is described as vulgar escapes me. Playful, flirtatious, frisky, and lighthearted, maybe, but definitely not vulgar. So, let's say for our purposes that nookie is, enjoying the intimate act of lovemaking (and everything leading up to it, lol) with your spouse. How's that sound? Make note of the playful, flirtatious, frisky, and lighthearted aspects... IMPORTANT stuff. Moving on!

How important do you think it is to have fun and enjoy your marriage? How much more important is it to have fun in the bedroom? (The fun, sexy times don't have to be limited to the bedroom, but more on that later) Though rhetorical, I believe you'd agree the answer to these questions are…VERY IMPORTANT. Life can be hellish (thank GOD He's everything)! and full of ups, downs, challenges, disappointments, responsibilities, bills, meetings, and more. So when it comes to your family, sanctuary, or lover, you just want to keep it light. So be LIGHT, in every sense of the word. Be playful toward each other, play with each other, be free to enjoy each other. Nookie with your mate is physical, emotional, and spiritual, and divine love should be at its center. Love on your mate wholeheartedly. Life is to be lived to the fullest. Don't take it for granted. The Bible says that the marital bed is undefiled (Hebrews 13:4 NKJV) so be free to share your love and your bodies (from head to toe), and just enjoy every experience like it's your first. If love is at the center of it all, how can it not be good? There may not be earth shattering orgasms every time but knowing you both are committed to keeping things alive and fresh and new will make every experience special. Enjoy and have Christ-centered fun!

First assignment! Answer these questions:

Is there a location in your home that you'd like to explore and have some fun? Think outside the box (and bedroom!). Dialogue with your spouse. What would they say? Are you inspired to try a new area tonight? Where?

What can you do to lighten the mood? Play a quick game? Any game will do to decompress from the day. Just think about some lighthearted fun, even if it's for 5 minutes! (15 minutes is better, though...)

Remember the freedom to enjoy one another is major. Do you feel "FREE" to enjoy? Talk about it. Why/why not? What's an activity that would free you of an inhibition that would enhance your overall sex life?

What can you do toward your spouse to show your flirtatious and frisky side today? (Think foreplay, which we will address later in the book.)

(This page is left blank intentionally to jot down some notes. Make up your own questions for your mate to answer!)

Chapter 2

The Prerequisite to Funning:
Mama Says "Clean It Up!"

Warning: don't get offended by the elementary nature of what I'm calling you out on in this chapter. If it doesn't apply to you, keep it moving. If you have to think twice about it, it probably DOES apply to you, so take heed!

I am not here to insult anyone's intelligence. However, my research in preparing this book proved that we cannot make assumptions about what folks know and what they don't know. Understand that people don't know what they don't know! Be patient, kind, and loving in your communication, understanding that you don't know everything so don't assume other people know the same things you do.

In doing my research, I found that people did not share the same ideas about hygiene and cleansing habits. The subject came up in various discussions with folks. We all have days when the physical body is not at its freshest. Some is natural to the nth degree (lol) depending on your level of activity and some is from lack of knowledge and understanding of how to take care of self properly, what works best with your body's chemistry, etc. Again, don't assume folks know what they don't know. If they haven't been taught the way you've been taught and it leads to them not being their freshest, then as their lover, approach the subject LOVINGLY. For hubby and I, JOKINGLY worked, lol. I recall hubby emanating something less than pleasing to my nose one evening, to which he was already rectifying as the shower was already running. He knew he was lighting up the room. One whiff and I was like, "Dad, you're a little tart!" and he burst into laughter and headed for the shower. When I had a super active day, I would chase him around the room with my armpit until he would finally and reluctantly give in and inhale deeply, LOL! It still makes me giggle. Cleanliness is important however, it's okay to have fun even in the midst of the funk! Our habits were strong and solid. We loved water and bathing. We knew how to handle our business.

Take the time to learn your lover intimately enough to know all their different tastes, smells, looks, etc. and to know what good and not-so-good days are to them. However, heed this warning... having a bad underwear day should never be acceptable. Burn them. Don't let your mate see them! It's not CUTE! When your mate looks at you, you don't want them to wonder, "is he/she having a bad underwear day today? Are there fuzz bunnies in their butt crack from using too much Charmin? Uggghhhh, what am I smelling? What the Philadelphia cream cheese?" Some pictures you just don't want your mate to paint in his or her mind when they think of you! No Shout "-ing" out the train tracks in your mates drawz! Don't you want your mate to think about you as sexy and edible? If so, do away with that issue ever being an issue! The things I found out during my research would blow your mind! I digress. I'll add, though, that you must consider the health aspects of not being clean and exposing your mate to bacteria, especially women, who may get infections (urinary tract infections and more) if you come to the party cheesy. Ok. I digress... again.

You must do the prework before you can get to the fun part of lovin. What do I mean? Do what you need to do to come correct to the lovin party and it's so important to communicate with your spouse and come to a shared understanding of what clean means to you as a couple. Prepare as best you can. There's nothing wrong with keeping some handy dandy moist towelettes on hand to eliminate the fuzz bunnies and any residual odorificness! (it's a made-up word, but you get my drift!). Change your soap or deodorant if you and your mate don't feel it's cutting the mustard.

Cleanliness is next to Godliness! This is a popular phrase but is this a thing, really? Well, in principle it is. Though the Bible doesn't say these words exactly, there are many references about the physical body being clean. (Reference Leviticus 17:15 – 16 and 2nd Kings 5:10). So, what is CLEAN? There are so many definitions, but for our purposes of intimate relations, let's agree that clean is "removing something unwanted that may potentially offend."

It's so important to communicate openly and honestly with your lover about your wants, needs, and desires and cleanliness is a part of that. Don't assume they KNOW or can read your mind and don't assume that your definition of clean is the same. Some people like stinky feet or a little more *au naturel* in the nether regions. That's all good, if that's what you like!

What am I saying? Let me break it down to you. In order to have fulfilling intimate experiences with your mate, you have to know what their expectations are (communicate, communicate, communicate!), and you must know if you are operating on the same understanding of that expectation (again, don't assume people know what they don't know! What means one thing to you may mean something totally different to someone else).

Note that I am in no way suggesting that nookie has to be rigid or structured. What I am suggesting is that you are considerate, respectful, and ready to please one another which MAY take some forethought or prework on your part. The prework is not just in the communication but also in the preparation.

Let's think about preparation and presentation. The prerequisite to getting freaky is, "Mama says clean it up! Wash yo' tail!" Think about those times of exploration where the sky is the limit. Don't you want you and your mate to explore knowing that you both have come correct? Make sure you keep your hygiene habits consistent and on the up and up. Clean your ears. Who wants to lick and/or suck an unclean ear or nibble a navel that smells of hot Limburger cheese? And don't forget your feet. Clean in between EACH toe and take special care to moisturize the bottom of your feet including your heels. Keep your hands, fingernails and toe nails clean and file those rough edges. No one wants Mr. or Mrs. Edward Scissorhands playing with the kitty or massaging the gonads! Shredded meat doesn't feel good.

"Cleanliness *IS* next to Godliness," so bathe! Come correct. Present your best self to your lover, especially when you want to do a lot of exploration and foreplay. Respect yourself and your partner enough by coming to the party squeaky clean. Natural odors are simply that… natural! Your level of activity will determine the intensity of your natural essence but, set the standard of freshness and cleanliness. Start with a clean slate, literally. It fosters an atmosphere for freely exploring one another. Don't allow yourself to be in a potentially embarrassing or offensive situation. The body's natural essence will emanate magnificently and perfectly throughout your playtime. That makes things all the more inviting and delicious when you can build that sexy scent together.

Think about this. You know when you have something that's REALLY good? You think, "Ooooooh, I can't wait to have THAT again!" That's what you want to feel when you think of intimacy with your boo-thang. The sight, smells, and tastes all leave an imprint on their brain. Make the memory desirous of more of that good thang.

Just think about how much more deliciously pleasurable your romps will be when you are operating under the same understanding and expectation. You can just wallow in the essence and juices of your nookie experience! You won't have to wonder, "what am I going to encounter today? Cheese? A floral bouquet? Sandalwood? Fish? Musk?" *Jesus, be at the helm of this ship, 'cause your funky people need some help! LOL*

Set out to tantalize and tickle the senses and get yourself ready for what is to come. Understand that what comes before the main event sets the stage for what's to come. Satisfy the prerequisite. And if you don't have the time to freshen up, you and your spouse can always bathe together! Revel in the smells of fragrant bath gels or earthy soaps and enjoy the feel of the thick lather running through your fingers as you bathe each other. If all goes well, you may not even make it to the bedroom!

Now I realize that some like a little stank on it – I get it! Who am I to say that's right or wrong? So, my advice would be to explore the flower petals and ocean breeze option first, decide what you do and don't like, communicate it, and go with it! Again, if roasted salty nuts or the seafood platter is your flavor of choice, go with the funky flow!

Just don't make assumptions.

Peace.

Chapter 3

Set the Dinner Table

For this reason, a man shall leave his father and mother and be joined to his wife, and the two shall become one flesh. This is a great mystery, but I speak concerning Christ and the church. Nevertheless, let each one of you in particular so love his own wife as himself, and let the wife see that she respects her husband." Ephesians 5:31 – 33 (NKJV)

Let's talk about "Setting Your Table," preparing for an encounter with your mate. This chapter is about considering the extra things your mate enjoys, or something new that may just pleasantly surprise you both.

Preparation packs a powerful punch when pleasing your partner in a paramount pleasure palace. (Try saying that five times fast!) You know those lovemaking sessions in your head that are experiences not yet fulfilled? They take a little planning, right? Keep these key words in mind: Preparation. Picture. Presentation. Precursor. Peak Performance. Permission. Patience. Persistence. Please. Pleasure. Plenty. Position. Praise.

Let's break it down. Preparation is essential for any future sexual experiences. Think about what you need to do to get that dreamed-of experience? Paint that picture. How will you lay it out? Is there anything you need to consider as far as props and atmosphere? Are you ready to perform? What do you need personally to pull it off? Is the sky the limit when it comes to experimenting or have you and your lover communicated about limits?

Patience is a must, of course, as the desires of your partner should be highly considered and vetted and should be important to you. Persistence is good, too. Keep doing what you're doing to invoke a positive response from your lover. Please them and make them ask for more. Be ready, especially if you introduce a new yummy position or technique. It's all about pleasing one another ultimately and looking forward to many more awesome and new experiences.

Last, but certainly not least... PRAISE. Praise your partner for work well done. Be thankful for the opportunity to share in such a wonderful experience with the love of your life knowing that God knows us better than we know ourselves and we are truly free to express it under the marriage covenant. Praise and thank God in ALL things!

So, how exciting is the preshow entertainment before the main event?! It helps get you moving, excited, and warms you up! (Don't judge me, it can be a party for Jesus!)

What about how beautiful the prelude to a song is? It's that auditory teaser that pulls you into a melodious space as you anticipate the next movement.

What I want you to think about here is what you need to do in preparation for what's to come later.

Picture this. You're invited to your friend's house for dinner who happens to be a great chef. You know the food is going to be the bomb! There's anticipation and excitement, right? Why? Because you know the chef is talented, passionate about what he does, knows what works and what doesn't flavor-wise and aesthetically, and he aims to please you, the guest. You arrive to a warm welcome. The atmosphere is amazing. Before dinner is served, you slam the delicious appetizer and anticipate what's to follow because you know it's going to be mind-blowing.

The preshow, prelude, and appetizer in the aforementioned are all important parts of the total package or experience. It's the preparation before you get to the main event. It sets the stage for what's to come.

I love painting pictures. Indulge me! Visualize this...

It's Thanksgiving. The dining table is set with the best china and silver, shined to perfection. The complimenting and contrasting colors of deeps reds, burnt orange, and chocolate browns dance like autumn leaves blowing across the sunny blue sky. The champagne flutes sit side by side with the water glasses and each napkin ring bears the design that can also be found on each plate. There are also vases of different heights on the table filled with fresh flowers that lightly perfume the air. The presentation lets you know that your host has thought of everything. It's beautiful.

It's almost dinnertime and your senses are alive! You are captivated by those familiar meal-time sounds as the clock ticks and you hear the pots and pans clanging and clamoring. The time is drawing near. The aroma of the turkey, candied yams, kale greens, macaroni and cheese, and yeast-risen rolls permeates every corner of the house. You smile in appreciation knowing your host planned the menu weeks ago and has spent the past few days shopping, basting, chopping, cooking, and everything else involved in preparing an unforgettable Thanksgiving experience.

Before you even lay eyes on it, you are anticipating your palate being tantalized by the delicious combination of sweet and savory flavors. Then, you see it. Your eyes dance in excitement and take in the myriad of colors -- the brown gravy on that succulent meat, the gooey, oozing, yellow cheese surrounding and entering the jumbo macaroni noodles, the beautiful dark, leafy greens laden with chunks and shards of smoky meat, and the glistening of the rich, buttery, cinnamon-topped yams. You salivate in anticipation of consuming it and the anticipation mounts with expectancy of what's to come. Your reaction is exactly what your host pictured and she smiles softly.

You can't wait to just taste and enjoy the explosion of flavors. Then you dip yo' finger in that brown gravy and "sluuuurp!" to suck your finger clean! Fireworks go off in your mouth and your taste buds leap and shout and that's just the beginning! You consume until your heart's content. You really don't want the experience to end, but when it does, you are thinking that you can't wait to experience that again. Before you fall asleep at the table, you turn to your host and with exuberance and gratitude praise her for her hard work, her dedication to detail, and for all the love she poured into the meal. Now that's a dining experience!

When you listen to a classical piece of music by a skilled pianist and the prelude strokes your eardrums, don't you close your eyes in anticipation of the next movement of the piece? (Maybe I'm just overly artistic....) The music toys with your emotions and heightens your senses. The sounds, the colors, the smells, the feel, if you would allow yourself the freedom to experience the fullness of the music, will transport you into the beautiful picture painted by the composer. Teleported to the scenery where you can smell the grass, touch the water in the brook, and see and hear the birds as they swoop, chirp, and drink of the nectar from the beautiful flowers, for instance... The music evokes different feelings as you listen to the crescendo and decrescendo of the music, watching fingers dance up and down the keyboard masterfully massaging the ivory. You're entangled and enraptured anticipating what's yet to come. The sounds and your emotions intensify to climax and its end, which leaves you feeling pleasantly full, connected, satiated, overjoyed, and complete. You rarely want it to end but when it does, you still want more. Until the next song takes you on that same trip or high but with a different experience.

The total experience or package is what you need to hone in on. All of this is to encourage you to think about your prework and preparation. Is your table set? What have you done to prepare and be ready for the sexual experience of your life? How is your presentation? Are you making yourself and the atmosphere look, smell, and feel enticing? Remember, praising your partner is important and boosts their confidence. Remind them of what you like. Make your dreams come true!

Communicating (always) and preparation are key. What helped me and other couples I know is to explore these questions:

- Do I know my mate's love language? There are 5: receiving gifts, quality time, words of affirmation, acts of service, and physical touch. (See References for more information!) Study them and know what makes your mate feel loved and appreciated. Do you know that's foreplay? When you can speak to what interests, motivates, encourages, pleases, etc. your mate, I'm here to tell you the juices flow, the panties (or drawz if that's what you wear) drop, and it's on like popcorn! Make your mate feel special and like they are the only person that matters to you in that time and space.
  - o Primary love language:
  - o Secondary love language:
  - o Identify and discuss similarities and differences.

- ■
- ■
- ■
- ■
- ■
- ■
- ■
- ■
- ■

- What physical act pleases my mate without penetration can I can expound on or hone in on for our next session? Is it sucking toes? Nibbling the thigh? Massaging the scalp? List some things to explore.
  - ○
  - ○
  - ○
  - ○
  - ○
  - ○
  - ○
  - ○

- What do you consider a normal sex life? (How long does a session need to last? How often do you want to have sex?) Does your idea match your spouse's? How can you both compromise to make sure you are both satisfied?

  o

  o

  o

  o

- What are some specific preferences

  o Where do you prefer to get busy? (For most men and some women I already know your answer…. ANYWHERE!)

  o Perfumed or *au naturel*?

  o What is your stance on using food during sex?

  o Do you prefer the lights on or off?

  o Temperature (steaming hot or the fan blowing)?

  o Favorite positions?

  o Bare or hairy?

  o How do you feel about giving and/or receiving oral pleasure?

  Now, come up with your own questions that you are curious about. Take the time to discuss them with your mate.

-
-
-
-
-
-
-
-
-
-

Ladies, let's be real for a moment, please. There are certain things that our men want from us, but we are reluctant to oblige them on a regular. You have to ask yourself, "why?" Do you have hang-ups when it comes to intimacy? Is there a reason why you don't want to know the person you are married to (for better or for worse, in sickness and in health, 'til death do y'all part) inside, outside, and upside down, too? Besides God, no one should know your man more intimately than you.

Men are simple. There are certain things that make them happy and these things are pretty easy and simple to accomplish if you go about them in the right spirit. In my experience, there are four things that a man likes stroked: His intellect, his ego, his palate, and his penis. Let's break it down.

- *His intellect*. Believe it or not, there are men who are very much turned on by a woman's intelligence. How and what she articulates and how her mind works is stimulating men who like their brain challenged. You can see their eyes light up when you challenge them with your prowess. For this man, if you can stimulate his mind, then and only then can you ride the wave.

- *His ego*. Ladies, sometimes you just have to bite the bullet. Boost him up. Tell him how wonderful he is. Let him beat on his big chest and proclaim "I Am MAN." Seriously, he must know and feel that he's the KING of his castle. It's your duty and responsibility to support him in his role as head of the household. If he's not quite there, do what you need to do as his other half to encourage him to take his rightful place as head of the house. Just remember, the head can't function without the neck and you're the neck! You are his helpmate. He depends on you to see those things he can't. Support and build him up when he's weak. This is a partnership. Your job as his wife is important. Take your rightful position, too! By all means, pray for your man, too. I saw great changes in my husband when I humbled myself and simply prayed for him. No nagging!

- **His palate.** This is easy if you can cook. If you can't, either learn or figure out how to feed that man! Give him some good food then rub his belly for him later.

- **His penis.** Since we are talking about spicing things up in the love life, let's be real. We have to be willing to work that thang, whatever that means to you and your lover. Do your best to please him the way he likes to be pleased. Just work it!

Now men, you are not exempt from this discussion. You have work to do, too! We know you have needs just like women. A lot of times, there is a direct correlation between your needs being met and a woman's emotional health when it comes to the relationship. As her head and covering, you have certain responsibilities to ensure she feels safe and secure, that you consider her emotions and reach her intimately without it always being about just sex, and that she feels loved and appreciated. Let's explore.

- **Safety and security.** She needs to trust your word and know that you have her back. She needs to feel safe under your headship and the decisions you make that affect her and the family.

- ***Intimacy without sex***. Sometimes, she just wants attention. Bathe her and give her impromptu foot and back rubs. Ask her about her day and be an attentive listener.
- ***Reassurance***. Show her affection, tell her and show her you love her.
- ***Appreciation***. Show appreciation by helping with the chores without her asking, and doing things that she would appreciate. Flowers? A surprise gift?

When Mama has a sense of emotional wellbeing, it will spill over into all areas of her life, especially intimacy and nookie. When Mama's happy, everybody's happy! Do your part as her man to ensure you're depositing into her emotional bank account, not depleting it.

Remember that you should not withhold intimacy, except for a mutually agreed-upon time for fasting and praying (1st Corinthians 7:4-5).

Do you have to know the answer to all your mate's preferences, likes, and dislikes? NOPE. But it surely is fun trying to figure them out. Preferences change and being connected and tuned in is necessary to keep your relationship flourishing. Discovery is fun! Some things you will learn about yourself and your boo-stanka from your experiences together. Try to find out these things in whichever way works best for you. Use these questions as a fun way to talk about your preferences or simply experiment and discover! Have any other questions peaked your curiosity that you'd like to find out about your lover? Write them down here and either ask or find interesting and fun ways to figure it out!

When getting ready for a night (or day) of passion, remember these three things at a minimum: preparation, presentation, and praise. It'll take you a long way in pleasing your mate!

(This space left blank intentionally for notes and questions!)

Chapter 4

Mind-Loving:
Foreplay Before Foreplay

"Wives, submit to your own husbands, as is fitting in the Lord. Husbands, love your wives and do not be bitter toward them." Colosians 3:18-19 (NKJV)

Let's talk foreplay. Why? Because it matters! It's a way to build the anticipation of what's to come. It's tantalizing, fun, and stimulating. You know a good lovemaking session starts in the mind first. It's not just the physical act of foreplay and intercourse, with touching, licking, and penetrating. It begins before intercourse and usually ends much later than the physical act. When you plant a seed, it needs food, water and light to grow and thrive. Plant that seed of intimacy early in the day so it can lead to delicious pleasures at night.

Think about your compatibility and your sex type. You are either stimulated through your mind and emotions or you are stimulated by what's physical. I typically find that men are visual and tend to be (and like) a more hands-on approach, the physical. Women tend to be more touched by feel-good, thoughtful expressions, matters of the heart, sensitive gestures, and so on. So ladies, do something or show him something to keep his motor revving throughout the day, and gentlemen, give her those "feel good" moments throughout the day. It'll do you well in the long run! Be creative! Some examples are:

- Leave a note in the briefcase.
- Leave a voicemail message on their office phone.
- Give them a lingering look or touch (grab dat booty or crotch!) as you leave for work.
- Whisper in their ear about what you want to do to them after work.
- Give them flowers or any other delivery during the day.
- Impromptu lunch date.

And the list goes on and on! Can you think of some way to tantalize and tease your lover today that will lead to a night of passion? Just use your imagination and let it flow and jot some things down!

-
-
-
-
-

-
-

Remember, the total experience goes above and beyond penetration.

Can I talk to the foodies real quick? (Can you tell I like food and feeding folk?) Don't you feel a certain amount of anticipation when you know you are about to eat something really good? Your tummy growls in anticipation. Your mouth salivates. Eating it is like heaven as you savor the flavors. You never want the deliciousness to end but when it does, you know you want it again.

There's something to be said about having some good stuff, whatever that stuff may be, and looking forward to experiencing it again. When you make love, it's about the total experience. Liken the above dining experience or musical experience to your sexual experience. There is a common thread. There is some "thing" that leads up to something else that makes the experience complete.

Now, am I to suggest that there must be a laundry list of things you must do BEFORE you get busy? Absolutely NOT! However, I will say that some things are a must and nonnegotiable. Communication is key throughout all aspects of your relationship. When it comes to intimacy, communication is IMPERATIVE, and preparation takes some forethought, vision, and a certain amount of planning.

Don't get stuck in a rut by having the same experience, same position, in the same place over and over again. Your relationship is for your lifetime! Keep it interesting and fun. It's not just a physical act. It starts in the mind first. Make love to your mate's mind and enhance the physical all the more.

What does your prework look like? Is your dining table set? Are you making love to your mate's mind today in preparation of tearing them up tonight? (and I mean that in a good way!)

Enjoying each other is the goal. Knowing how to bring about the enjoyment or pleasure is where you need to do your homework. Again, be free to communicate your likes and dislikes. Explore and discover new things about each other. Oh, you like salt instead of sugar on your grits? Well, if you like a little salt on the situation, and that's your collective stance on the matter, then by all means, go salty! Who am I to say differently? What I encourage always is to communicate and decide what you like and dislike. Preferences are important factors to know and consider when planning playtime.

Chapter 5

Foreplay:
Licky-Licky Before the Sticky-Sticky

Now, let's really talk FOREPLAY, the purely physical kind. Kiss me. Touch me. Stroke me. Feel me. Inhale me. Taste me. Tease me. Nibble me. Talk me through it. Now do it all again and again!

Foreplay is an amazing way to learn one another's bodies, sensitive spots and hot spots and can build on the total lovemaking experience. Kissing the body and tasting each other is just a part of it. Who says you can't enjoy oral? As a Christian, I've heard so many frigid, restrictive untruths about what should and should not be done. There is FREEDOM in living a Godly, married life. NO restrictions!

Kissing is a natural way of showing love and affection toward your lover. Kissing does not stop at the lips on your face but can be enjoyed all over the body. Oral foreplay is a delicious experience and feels different from touching with your finger or hands to both parties involved. It's about perspective. Learning your lover's body from a different perspective can be fun and enjoyable and enlightening. It's not just about the touch and response, but you must look, listen, smell, and taste. Drink it all in to experience your mate fully. Learn what feels good to them. Don't be shy! Ask questions, give directions, point, demonstrate, try a different technique – circle, swirl, twirl, suck, zig zag, squeeze – whatever floats the boat!

What are some other physical acts of foreplay that would be fun to explore?

- *Make out.* There's nothing like a good make-out session to heighten your desire for one another. Decide this day to spend extra time simply enjoying kissing each other. Kisses are so special. Don't take this art form lightly! Set a timer. Try a 10-minute, lip-locking, tongue dance, varying in force, pressure, technique – you know what to do!
- *Don't touch!* Just say no. Teasing is one of the biggest turn-ons. Playfully give the 'no-no' look and run! You are sure to be followed. Your partner will make you give and that's what you want anyway!
- *Massage.* The power of touch is healing in so many ways. If you want to show your lover you care, a massage is a must. It's healthy, rejuvenating, relaxing, stress-relieving, and

it's SEXY. A simple back or foot massage can lead to a butt or thigh massage. That'll heat things up. Destress then release. Sounds like double the pleasure to me!

- ***Good, old-fashioned spooning.*** It's such a loving and warm feeling to just cradle each other. The way the arch of a woman's back lays against his gut and her booty nestles right in his crotch? Just comfortable familiarity, right? Wiggle a couple of times, and it's off to the races!

- ***Mutual undress.*** Ask if you can undress your partner today. Take your time. Allow your fingers and hands, and even your mouth, to lightly touch the skin as you undress. Juices begin to flow and soldiers stand at attention! This is a sure-fire way to start your evening.

- ***Food play.*** What's for dinner? Or, maybe dessert? Incorporating food in your foreplay (and even in lovemaking) can be so much fun! Chill a berry and share from mouth to mouth. Pull out the caramel and whipped cream. The sky is the limit. Hey, if you like cheese, pull it out and make a cheese and fruit display on your mate and as you eat it off, share nibbly bits mouth to mouth.

- ***Follow the leader.*** Do you normally take the lead? Are you the initiator or dominator? Well, change it up from time to time. Your mate will be pleasantly stunned if you grab hold to those reigns and dominate! Grab your mate by the hand and lead him/her on a follow the leader excursion around the house. Call the shots!

- *Blindfolded "love"-capades.* Oh, this fun game is scintillating, sexy, and sensual. Blindfold your mate, which will cause all the other senses to heighten. They won't know what's coming at them next – a smell, a food, a sensation from some external stimuli, like a feather, a wand, something warm, something wet. Let your imagination go wild! Your mate's sensitivity to whatever you present is highest at this point!

- *Learn something new together.* When was the last time you did something totally new together? Like a new dance move? Or a new recipe to cook together? The bond created while sharing in a new experience is something you cannot minimize and nothing can take that away. Try something new today. It will translate into a new experience in the bedroom and is definitely foreplay. The closeness of bodies, the smell of heat when you're dancing and the taste of each other's fingers while sample a recipe can lead to all kinds of naughty things.

- ***Find the "P" (punani/penis).*** How's that for Hide and Go Seek? Leave some clues around the house for your mate to find the goodies!

We can take the last bullet a step further. What's punani? Well, the word originally means a Hawaiian heavenly flower. Well, for our purposes and how it's commonly used is the woman's "heavenly flower" if you get my drift. I know this may be a stretch for some, but indulge me here. Let's say, ladies, you really want to spice things up. How about a punani platter?! How about we call it the "pu-pu" platter! I know most are familiar with that delicious delectable platter of appetizer-type small-bite finger foods (foodies know what I'm talking about) that cause you taste buds to orgasm called the pu-pu platter. Let me encourage you to try this out! Make your own pu-pu platter for your man!

If you are wondering the specifics, let your mind wander and create a pu-pu platter suitable for your mate's taste buds! Assemble atop your nether region some tasty treats, snack foods, or a full mashed potato bar with toppings if that is his (and your) pleasure! Prepare your goodies in advance because once you start building your platter, you won't be able to get up without disrupting your creation! You are the base of your creation! You are his platter of deliciousness!

Now, fellas, you are not exempt. You can be your wife's pu-pu platter, too! The same thing applies as above. You can BE her sundae on Sunday night! You already possess the banana and nuts! (Sorry, I just couldn't pass up that opportunity!) You get my drift though. Layer your nether-land with her favs and you will tickle her palate and she will devour and arouse. You may just get that special treat that you only get on special occasions! LOL. Double the pleasure and fun!

Now, what are you thinking? Are your creative juices flowing? Write down some ways to incorporate other forms of foreplay in your sexual existence with your love. Be imaginative. Try to outdo each other. That's a game in itself that leads to a lighter, loving, more intimate existence.

(This space intentionally left blank for foreplay notes!)

Chapter 6

Get Your Freak On!

"Who can find a virtuous wife? For her worth is far above rubies. The heart of her husband safely trusts her; so he will have no lack of gain. She does him good and not evil all the days of her life." Proverbs 31:10-12 (NKJV)

"Drink water from your own cistern and running water from your own well. Should your fountains be dispersed abroad, streams of water in the streets? Let them be only your own, and not for strangers with you. Let your fountain be blessed, and rejoice with the wife of your youth. As a loving deer and a graceful doe, let her breasts satisfy you at all times; and always be enraptured with her love. For why should you, my son, be enraptured by an immoral woman, and be embraced in the arms of a seductress? For the ways of man are before the eyes of the Lord, and He ponders all his paths. His own iniquities entrap the wicked man, and he is caught in the cords of his sin. He shall die for lack of instruction and in the greatness of his folly he shall go astray. Proverbs 5:15 – 23 (NKJV)

We presented our best selves, we teased each other into oblivion with the mental and physical foreplay, the motors are revving with some high octane fuel, juices are flowing, and our bodies are sensitive and throbbing with desire for each other. The time is now. It's time for the romp. It's time for the penetration. It's time for rocking, reeling, and rolling. It's time for riding, sliding and gliding! It's time for explosion after miraculous explosion. You know God is awesome the way He made our bodies. Can I get an Amen on that? It's time to get your FREAK ON!

Enjoy your mate physically. You have God's permission to enjoy the intimacy shared between husband and wife. Know, though, that loving your spouse freely is Godly! Again, you are with your spouse. No limits. No rules. Do what is acceptable before God under the covenant of marriage with the intention of pleasing one another. Be a freak for your mate!

So, what is freaky? It can mean odd, strange, unusual, or eccentric. It can also mean promiscuous, kinky, and sexually adventurous. For our purposes, let's agree that freaky means, "adventurous when relating to your spouse intimately and sexually." Now that we've established that, let's move on.

I recently heard a story on a popular daytime TV talk show. "Couples" was the topic and spicing things up in the bedroom was the challenge. There was a man who used to sing love songs to his bae, and their loving was great. Once the man got more involved in church, a lot of what pleased his wife fell by the wayside. She wanted her old stud muffin back! He was uncomfortable with singing the love songs to his wife AND being Godly, too.

In abandoning singing to his wife, he missed out on an important and simple way of loving and pleasing her. He said, "but, God is watching" as his excuse. Duh. Of course God is watching. He always has and He always will. Just because the husband now sings gospel music in church doesn't mean he can't sing love songs to his wife in the privacy of their inner sanctum.

People, my Bible tells me the marital bed is undefiled. Keep your love life alive! Keep it new, fresh, and exciting. Set out to please one another. Try whatever position that brings you both pleasure. There is no taboo position and no body part off limits for kissing. Love songs between you and your spouse in your inner sanctum is lovely. Your marriage was a vow taken before God and ordained by Him. He knows all about you anyway. Go forth and enjoy one another FREELY. Get freaky and be free!

Now, in the heat of the moment, forget the extra salt and the little bit of cheese. If you want it as you walk in the door from work, and the passion is undeniably high, strip at the front door and do the dang thang. Just throw caution to the wind and get your freak on. *Bwahahahahah!* It'll be memorable, that's for sure!

Can I share how wonderful my hubby was? My husband came hygienically correct, especially when I dropped hints and clues throughout the day. He would tidy up before leaving work so that if I wanted some nookie at the front door, or if I wanted to treat him to a special treat at the front door, he was READY! LOL. Take the hint! Know your partner. Bring it and come correct! Mama's gonna sit down now. Lol

Chapter 7

The Love Story

"Do not deprive one another except with consent for a time, that you may give yourself to fasting and prayer; and come together again so that Satan does not tempt you because of your lack of self-control." 1ˢᵗ Corinthians 7:5 (NKJV)

This is where it all began. The first glance. The first sighting. The moment you realized he or she existed. Your heart skipped a beat. Your tummy churned. There was a glow. A light. God whispered, "that's your future." Or maybe it wasn't that obvious from day one. Maybe it took a couple of dates and a few encounters before you realized that person was the one for you. Whatever the scenario, it brought you to this point.

There was something that brought you to this point of having a committed life partner and a family all your own. Are you thriving or are you existing as a couple? What brought you together? How did you meet? Where? Do you remember what he or she was wearing? What stood out? Did you feel an energy unlike any before? Don't forget those things that brought you together. These just may be the things you draw on to remember the "why?" when you have to pick up dirty socks off the floor, drop the toilet seat down, or clean hair out the drain.

As I sit and look at his picture, I think back to our story and how we came to be a couple. It wasn't love at first sight by a long shot. In the beginning, I couldn't even stand the sight of him! You heard me correctly, I didn't even like him! Repulsed was more like it. His 5'8" stature, round belly, greasy looking muddy water complexion, bamma blue tie-dye t-shirt and red, black, and white turned-up toe high-top British Knights did nothing to turn me on. Then there was the South Carolina accent with all the country slang that went along with it. Lord, help him. Help me! I knew what I liked -- 6'4", muscular, blue-black (or blurple) skin – you know the type. That was my type. God has a sense of humor, though.

He asked me to lunch. I hemmed and hawed, but he was persistent. I told my girlfriends that since he was nine years my senior, he might give me worms! Ugh. I reluctantly conceded with the stipulation that I bring my girlfriend along. So, for two weeks straight, we had lunch every day with my girlfriend in tow. He demonstrated GREAT patience (like, what man would do that?) He was special. This was the birth of our love affair.

Fast forward one year and my whole perspective has changed. I'm in love with this man. His skin? Like a Reese's buttercup and his body is sexy as ever with those broad shoulders and narrow waist. He's a southern gentleman, who is kind and gentle, and has the patience of the Biblical character *[1] Job when it comes to me. Wow, what a difference a year made. God will help you to see things that aren't visible initially, and He'll change your perspective. I can testify!

Fast forward a few more years and we are married with children. We're dealing with daycare, work, church and ministry, hectic schedules, and long commutes, uggghhh. We are so tired and before going to bed at night, we'd look at each other and say, "you good?" The other would reply, "Yeah, I'm good. Love you." "Love you, too. Good night." Life had gotten in the way and after three months of putting everything else in our life first, we finally planned intimate time together.

We were off to the races! The story above is an example of what you don't want to happen in your marriage, going

---
[1] *See Author's References

three months without nookie. It's the daily grind I'm speaking of. For those of you with children (daycare, softball, girl scouts), who work inside the home (yes, homemakers work hard, too) or outside the home and commute, have extracurricular activities (PTA, ministry meetings, and the list goes on!), does this sound all too familiar? Is the hustle and bustle of life depleting you of so much of your energy that you don't have time for one another?

Three months with no nookie? That was the first and last time for that madness. It sounds absurd to me now as I reflect. However, it happens. This should absolutely NOT be the norm. We were so wrapped up in everything else in life at the time that we didn't make our love life a priority. I don't think we even realized it had been so long, because we were so consumed with everything else in life. We were so burned out, we had no energy and sleep was more important than even a quickie.

I chuckle now because we definitely made up for it (and then some)! I'm so thankful that we both operated with patience and love toward each other without an expectation of "making it happen" at that time. There was no pressure from either of us to perform. This was not normal for us, but it was our life for that short period of time. Make sure this does not happen to you. Life will happen no matter what. Don't forget to take time for each other. Lovingly hold each other accountable.

Are you guilty? Are you enjoying good nookie regularly? What are you doing about it? Are you nurturing the relationship? Are you going through a dry spell and what are you doing about it? Are you ready to get the flame back and burn with desire for his or her touch? Do something now and consider incorporating something new into your love life! Don't let the opportunity to love one another pass you by. Don't allow the pressures of life to keep you from nurturing your relationship. Make sure you find a way to show love and gratitude every day to your spouse. When I think of my husband, I think if I could just kiss him. Hold his hand. Spoon with him in bed. Or make love to him just one more time.

If you are new to marriage, you have a jump on things! Don't fall into the rut. Learn from the mistakes of those couples before you. Research, read, study, experiment, and know that nurturing your relationship is a priority and a must. Strive to please each other freely when sharing intimately. Get to know one another intimately through exploration and communication. This is not taboo – sex them up!

If you are not so new to marriage and you feel things could be spicier, I'd say go back to the very beginning. What was it that made you fall in love? Was it her beautiful smile? His intelligence? Her wit? Was it his swag? Her meekness or her strength? His shyness or his confidence? Was it the passion for God and life that pulled on you? Was it his hard body or the curve of her hips? Remember the beginning and those wonderful feelings you felt toward one another and those qualities you saw in each other. Fall in love all over again and don't let that flame go out! Remember those things that drew you. Don't let the hustle and bustle of life rob you of precious moments you could have with your lover. Remember to always have grace without the expectation of your mate performing perfectly. Focus on the positive and praise the positive (and this applies in every aspect of your relationship).

Chapter 8

A Little Dab'll Do Ya

"Let the husband render to his wife the affection due her, and likewise also the wife to her husband. The wife does not have authority over her own body, but the husband does. And likewise the husband does not have authority over his own body, but the wife does." 1ˢᵗ Corinthians 7:3-4 (NKJV)

What am I talking about here other than QUICKIES. When I speak of quickies, I'm not just speaking of the physical act of intercourse (ain't nuttin wrong with a quickie! lol) but also quick and easy tips for showing your mate your desire for connectivity, closeness, and nurturing the relationship. What have you done lately to spice things up and move forward in nurturing your relationship? Haven't you heard that it's the little things in life that matter? In a relationship, the little or simplest things could have the biggest impact. Are you willing to put in a little work?

Anything worth having is worth working for, right? I think intimacy and sex are the easiest in the relationship when you consider all the other hurdles in a marriage (money, trust, child rearing, accountability, and so on). Besides the relationship between you and God, your marriage should have top priority. Nurturing your marriage is important, but it doesn't have to be hard. However, you MUST be willing to put forth SOME effort and energy. I'm no physicist, but this is how I see it: No activity is possible without energy. It takes energy to make things work and move things positively or negatively (of course, in this case, we are talking about moving positively or moving forward in the relationship in unity, i.e., as a unit). In a unit, you have working parts and when operating as a unit, energy is transferred from one part(ner) to another part(ner) to make something else happen (cause and effect?). There is a connectivity between the working parts that causes the outcome. Now there are times when parts in a unit weaken and even fail and this causes some type of disconnect. This affects the overall performance of the unit as a whole. For a unit to work properly, efficiently, and effectively, connectivity must be present along with scheduled maintenance for the unit. Can you see the connection between energy, working parts, the unit as a whole, connectivity, and the importance of maintenance? Maybe this story will make it easier to understand. You know I love a good story.

The phone rings and even though I don't recognize the number, I reluctantly answer. "Hi, Sandy" they say like they know me. "This is Rick from XXX Heating and Cooling Company. How are you today?" Ugghh, big mistake. I shouldn't have answered! My mind is screaming in my own head, "here we go again! Doggone telemarketers." With my eyes rolled all the way up in my eye sockets, I respond, "I'm well, thanks, Rick. How can I help you?" "Well, Sandy, (dude, you don't know me) it's that time of year to have your air conditioning unit looked at and we are running a special..." and before he could finish his sentence, I interrupted with one long run-on sentence, "well, Rick, I just purchased a new unit just last year, so I'm good, but thanks anyway and you have a great day!" Click. I felt good about ending the conversation before the telemarketer could waste any more of my time. Yay me!

A month later, my air conditioning unit went out. Ha-ha, the joke's on me. So when the company came out to see what the problem was, I said, "...but my unit is only a year old, so I thought I'd be good for a while." The serviceman said, "Ma'am... (like he was annoyed with me... hmph!) it's called maintenance. If you want your unit to run efficiently, ma'am, it must be well maintained. You don't wait 'til it's broken." *Duh! Didn't I feel stupid.*

Ding, ding, ding.... I got it! Did you? Although this story has nothing to do with intimacy (though I felt intimately connected to my air conditioner when I was talking to it because it failed me... and don't judge me or act like you don't know what I'm talking about), there IS a correlation! The moral of the story is don't wait 'til it breaks to try to fix it. If I want cold air in the summer and warm air in the winter, I need to have my unit assessed and maintained to make sure it operates smoothly. In your love life, you must exert a little energy to maintain a level of connectivity of the working parts (partners) to keep the unity or unit operating smoothly. High five on that!

So now we know we have to put forth a little energy for those sparks to fly and keep that flame dancing (remember, this is the fun and easy part in the marriage), so let's move on to making time to do it.

Is finding time for intimacy a real issue? If you can manage fulfilling your duties and responsibilities with your various ministries, planning for, scheduling, and attending this meeting and that one, serving on this committee and volunteering for that group, then surely you can find time for your significant other. This is your better half, your ace in the hole, main support system, the one who prays for you daily, your support system, etc. You get the picture.

I understand that life happens and I know we get busy with everything it deals us. Just as we schedule and plan our lives for ministry, work, and the kids' activities, it's just as important to plan special moments to keep the romance going with your spouse. Here are some very easy and quick ways to keep that connection going and fan that flame. A little dab of this and a little sprinkle of that will do wonders. These are ALL easy enough to incorporate in your daily lives and calendar planning to give that flame some oxygen!

- *Date Night.* Your relationship with your spouse is important so this must be a priority on your calendar! Take a look at your calendar and plan your monthly, or weekly, date night months in advance. Will you need to be a little flexible? Absolutely. Will the date change? It very well may. However, it's an important meeting that should have a regular occurrence on your schedule. Try scheduling it earlier in the month so you have time to reschedule it should there be a VERY important, can't-get-outta-that-obligation kind of occurrence. Make sure you weigh it carefully, though. Your spouse may be considerate and understanding of your obligations, but don't put your boo on the back burner for just anything.

So, what does date night look like? Anything you want it to! It doesn't matter what time of day or night you do it, and it doesn't always require you to leave the house. It's simply about setting aside some mutually agreed upon time regularly to nurture your relationship. You can alternate from month to month who is responsible for making the plans. Be creative! It can be something in or outside the home. It can be a mutually agreed upon activity or a surprise for your spouse. This monthly or weekly date doesn't have to be about just sexing each other up (though it could be the wonderful ending to the date). What about hiring someone else to cook for you all and serving you both a candlelit meal in the confines of your home? Consider going to your favorite gospel artist's concert or a comedy show. What about dinner and dancing or a night at the theatre (and I'm not just talking the movie theater, but that works, too! Consider a play or musical from time to time.). How about a pottery or cooking class? Reading a book to one another? Getting a couple's massage? Attending a night of spoken word? All of these things can be extremely sensual and intimate and enhance your connection, which can lead to intimacy when it's all said and done. Can you think of some things you and your spouse would like to do together? What about some activity or event that you'd like to surprise your boo with? However you choose to plan, make notes and transfer them to your calendar. Date nights can turn into nookie nights but doesn't have to take the place of nookie nights. Sex is good and a the release is a stress reliever. Don't limit the fun.

- ***Nookie nights and quickie sessions.*** Nookie nights are those sessions where you plan to be intimate. There's good foreplay and you make the time to explore and have fun. They tend to be much longer than a quickie. A quickie is a quickie and really needs no explanation other than you're in and out, and oh, what a relief it is! Lol.

So...to plan or not to plan? That is the question! There is a lot to be said about spontaneity; however, when it comes to getting it in, you gotta get it in, right? You have a responsibility and duty to your spouse, and it's healthy and satisfying. What's wrong with having standing yummy nookie nights? That doesn't mean you can't have spontaneous romps, too. Have a discussion about what a healthy sex life looks like for you and your spouse. Let me tell you from experience, no matter how tired, drained, stressed, or overwhelmed I may be, I've never had a tryst with my husband that didn't make me feel better. Sex is great for relieving tension and stress, and it's good exercise, too! (Get that heart rate going!) So no matter how tired, drained, stressed, or overwhelmed you may be, sharing some planned intimate time with your lover is a good thing and has its advantages (and don't forget your body is not your own once you say "I do!" The two shall become one flesh, remember?)

Planning intimacy is important. We plan to do a lot of things regularly like going to the gym, spa, barber shop, etc. Don't you plan to visit Ray, Joe Bob, and Cousin Sue? So, when it comes to spending time with your spouse to nurture your relationship, don't you think that it is equally if not more important to schedule some sexy time? Are Tuesdays and Saturdays best? Or Mondays, Wednesdays, and Fridays? There's nothing wrong with planning time to be with your spouse. Be reasonable in your expectations and make sure that the times you agree upon, you hold to as best you can. If you're not in the habit of breaking appointments and you are always accountable to everyone else, be sure to treat your scheduled time with your spouse the same. Be reasonable, considerate, and selfless when dealing with your partner and your schedules and the time you set aside for one another. If you both embrace this, you can execute your nookie nights seamlessly. Once a week may be the norm for one couple whereas daily is the norm for another. Having an understanding of each other's needs, desires, and expectations and reasonably working toward fulfilling them in love is what is important. The bottom line is plan some good nookie time. Whether it's once, twice, or three times a week, spend some time physically loving on each other regularly.

Can some of these be quickies? Well, why not? It's your sex life. Do whatever is pleasing and acceptable to you both. It's hard to pre-plan those quickies sometimes, but make sure you capitalize on those few free moments in between meetings, while the kids are out playing, or before they get home. Just think outside the box and by all means, have fun with it. There is nothing wrong with that impromptu satisfying quickie! Some of the best, passionate encounters that I had with my husband were quickies. Check out these memories

The kids stepped outside and were in the front playing. They kept going in and out of the house and could appear, literally, at any second. However, this was a window of opportunity to connect and we seized the moment! After

locking the bedroom door...three minutes of pumping and sweating! AMAZING! WOW! Risky, and fun. We needed that release and what a stress reliever! <>

Another time when the kids were playing out front and I called to my husband, "Bae, the kids are out front with their friends. I need your help with something. Can you come here for a minute?" He walked in, saw me with my panties on the floor, shaking what my mama gave me. He stood there "at attention" and it was on like pop, pop, poppity popcorn! <>

On another morning, the house was quiet and I was taking a shower. I heard the bathroom door open and close, and I knew it was him. I felt a hand on my shoulder right before he joined me and began lathering me from head to toe. I turned and did the same for him. What came next was nothing less than delightful. <>

Another time, we rode home from the city together after a busy day at work. He was driving and I nodded off to sleep for a few moments to decompress from the day. I was lulled by the music and the sound of the tires caressing the road. I woke up and reached over to hold his hand. The tension from work was high today but this drive together made me forget all about that. He said, "Baby, you're beautiful" and I felt desire course through my loins. We picked up the kids from daycare, got them started with their homework, and explained to them that we'll review their homework with them in a few minutes after we go upstairs and get settled. Settled? NOT! There's nothing like a quickie after a rough day! <>

Do you get the picture? A quickie may take a little forethought or not. All you need is a few minutes, a small window of opportunity to have some spontaneous fun. It spices up the love life tremendously and helps a couple to stay connected. Again, it doesn't solve all problems, but when you are less tense, it surely helps you communicate and relate to each other more lovingly. Are you now considering ways to incorporate some quickies? Well, here are a couple suggestions.

- ***Surprises!*** Who doesn't like to be pleasantly surprised? Well, I know there may be some people who absolutely don't like them, but you know your spouse well enough to know whether they like them or not and what would be appreciated. I love surprises, and they can come in many forms.

Walking through the department store, I notice him eyeing a shirt. I thought, "that'll look good on him!" He went back to it a couple times to check it out but walked out the store without it. The next day, I stopped by the store on the way home to purchase it. I left it where he would see it once he settled in after work. From the other room, I heard him exclaim, "oh my goodness, babe! Thank you! I love it." I smile. Making him happy makes me happy. <>

He left for work and I picked up the phone to leave him a voicemail that was waiting for him when he got to the office. "Baby, I know it's early and you're on your way to work, but I just wanted to leave you this message to let you know I can't wait to see you this evening when you get home. You left the house this morning looking good enough to eat. I love you and have a wonderful day." <>

Chocolate-covered strawberries are our favorite. The box of the tasty treats were left on the pillow with a note: "For our pillow talk tonight, lover." <.>

Do these get you thinking about little surprises for your lover? These little acts make your lover feel special, thought of, and loved. It's fun and stimulating, too, and can lead to an intimate exchange. Keep an open mind and be creative. Know what your partner likes and show appreciation in simple, subtle ways.

Date nights, nookie nights, and surprises can all be a part of your schedule and plan to spice up your love life. As I said before, if you can take time to plan other aspects of your life you can surely make a habit of planning aspects of your love life. Nurturing this relationship is important and that's why adding date nights to the calendar is necessary. Do YOUR part. Including the topics and scenarios outlined above, consider penciling in your calendar things like: pillow talk, leaving a note in his briefcase, picking up flowers on the way home, fixing his favorite meal tonight, drawing a bubble bath for you both after the kids go to bed, and the list goes on and on.

Making time for your spouse is important. When you understand your spouse's needs, desires, and wants and are sensitive to those things, your spouse will feel appreciated. They will feel special, like a priority in your life, and will feel truly loved by you. All of these bring about a sense of wellbeing, contentment, and happiness in your relationship. You'll find yourself wanting to "out do" each other in pleasing each other in ways you hadn't previously considered. Doesn't that sound exciting? Never a dull moment, right? Remember, your relationship with your spouse requires maintenance and a certain level of connectivity to work. Ain't nothin' to it but to do it!

- ***Bedtime is bedtime.*** For me, this is an important quick fix to intimacy. My husband and I went to bed together, at the same time, most nights. This is an easy quick fix to maintaining a level of connectivity. Laying down together is an opportunity to recap the day, have pillow talk, look into each other's eyes, lovingly caress, and drift into an exhaustive sleep after a long day, with or without lovemaking. If you are off doing other things before bedtime, have an agreed-upon target time to come to bed daily, conventional schedules permitting. It may change from day to day. You may agree to go to bed together twice a week. Just know that going to bed together is an option for connecting, especially when schedules are hectic.

Can you think of some other quick and easy ways to show appreciation, gratitude, and connectivity with your spouse? Jot them down here.

(This page is left blank intentionally for notes!)

Chapter 9

Trips, Toys, Timbs, and Tasty Treats

"Little children, keep yourselves from idols." 1st *John 5:21 (KJV)*

"Wives, submit to your own husbands, as to the Lord. For the husband is head of the wife, as also Christ is head of the church; and He is the Savior of the body. Therefore, just as the church is subject to Christ, so let the wives be to their own husbands in everything. Husbands, love your wives, just as Christ also loved the church and gave Himself for her, that He might sanctify and cleanse her with the washing of water by the word, that He might present her to Himself a glorious church, not having spot or wrinkle or any such thing, but that she should be holy and without blemish. So husbands ought to love their own wives as their own bodies; he who loves his wife loves himself." *Ephesians 5:22-28 (NKJV)*

I was working in my DC office but I couldn't get my mind off my stud muffin. Just the thought of him and all his talents *sent a shiver down my spine. I quivered at the anticipation of seeing him later, mmm mmmm mmmmmm; knowing that he knows just what to do and my wanting him to do it. I placed that mid-day call to him and whispered, "I got a surprise for you" in my sing-songy yet sensual way. I giggled and hung up the phone knowing that he wondered what I was up to, and his temperature was rising.*

That evening, I set the mood and had the atmosphere reeking of love and passion. I beat him home so I could prepare after dropping the kids off at Nanny's house. (She was my ace in the whole, God rest her soul.) Candles lit? Check Food cooking? Check. Skin-tight body suit on? Check. I heard the key in the door, so I ran to the kitchen to pop a large strawberry in my mouth for him to eat from my mouth. I greeted him with a delicious deep kiss as we devoured the strawberry together. The look in his eyes told me he was hungry and it wasn't for his favorite meal of fried chicken, pinto beans, and corn bread that was in the kitchen. Daddy had a sweet tooth that night! I was his dessert before dinner. I remember thinking, "Tonight, I'm treating HIM, it's not about me." As I made my move to devour him, he managed to ask, "Where are the kids?" as his eyes rolled back in his head. We never made it past the front door. <>

My phone call midday was the foreplay to what ended up being a memorable nookie session! I fulfilled a fantasy that he didn't even know he had! All sessions should be memorable but there's got to be effort sometimes for some extra special planning and loving. Don't allow your love life to become mundane and boring. Spontaneity is awesome, and I'm not taking away from those amazing quickie sessions, but there is something to be said about that thought out, planned out, and executed romp. For the scenario above, the foreplay was a mental tease that started the motors revving early in the day which carried into the evening after work. I called him and gave him something to think about.

"Hi Daddy, I'm Candy." *Candy is the long blonde-haired alter ego. She loves to wear lace and stilettos and has a prominent beauty mark above her lip. Daddy's got a sweet tooth tonight and Candy is sure to satisfy it. <>*

Can you imagine what your lover's mind is doing when that phone call comes in? Whether it's Candy or Tarzan and Jane doing their jungle call, role playing can also be great stimuli for you and can be really interesting and exciting foreplay. Have fun and play dress up sometimes. Ladies, play with wigs! It's fun. You and your mate can name each of them and define the characteristics of each... or NOT! Ladies, don't you think it will be fun to introduce your new character? Men, though you may not want to wear a wig, but no judgement if you do, *bwahahahahahah*, are there certain uniforms or other props you'd like to introduce? Keep the creative juices flowing! You can even talk about a scenario that you'd like to play out with each other. For instance:

Jack entered the establishment and was strapping in his well-made tailored suit. Though dimly lit, he saw her across the room -- the most beautiful lady he'd ever laid eyes on. He sat back and admired her beauty for a few minutes. Her dark brown coiffed hair, her naturally pouty lips that she accentuated with every draw on the straw as she sipped her iced tea, her lovely delicate, expertly manicured fingers toyed with jewels around her neck all caught his attention. His eyes drunk in the very essence of her being. She turned to meet his gaze as he strutted toward her. Without a word, he reached for her hand, pulled her to her feet, and they danced the night away. They never once uttered a word. They were mesmerized by the music and the familiarity with one another, though they had not formally introduced themselves. At the end of the last dance, he kissed her cheek, and they parted ways as strangers in the night. <>

Joe who has never served as a fireman, enters the room this night dressed in fireman gear, hose and all! He proclaims, "Ma'am, I'm here to rescue you and put out your fire!" She gasps as she sees him, now realizing that something is missing from his uniform as he stands at attention! "What a sight to see," she giggles. <>

You and your spouse can create different scenarios for your monthly date night. Think outside the box to stimulate creativity in your relationship. What have you done lately to stimulate your partner mentally? Are you open to role playing? Do you know what your lover may want to explore? What are those things? Have you shared your desires lately, because they DO change? These are things that you should discuss. Sounds like a good discussion for pillow talk, don't you think so? Be open, honest, and free in your communication and expressions of love. For instance, "I like it when you do XYZ to me." "When you do XYZ, it makes me want to do XYZ." Just talking about it may spark something tonight. Create a role play scenario together.

(This page intentionally left blank for notes.)

Another story? Yes….

It was my husband's birthday. I knew he was excited, not just because the Lord saw fit for him to see another day and another year, but also because he knew the birthday treats would be in abundance. Presents were in order for the King of the Castle, which included a toy crown and intangible things that he hadn't had in a while but he knew he would get because he was the birthday boy. In addition to that, he opened his birthday envelope and was excited to see COOCHIE COUPONS! He was overjoyed and I giggled. I knew he was thinking "not only can I get my birthday "special treat" but now I can get certain treats by redeeming my coupons!"

- *Toys*

Now if there was ever a taboo subject in the Christian existence, it's toys. What are the limits? What's acceptable? I cannot determine for you what is right or wrong, acceptable or not. In all things, seek God. If you have to question if it's beyond the limit of what's acceptable, it probably is. Ask yourself, "Would God be pleased if…?" You have to be careful as to not "idolize" things you introduce into your union, your sacred bed. The Bible speaks clearly about worshipping false idols. (See Ezekiel 23:7, 20:24, 23:30, 36:18, 6:9; 16:36, 16:20, 14:3 – 4, 20:8; Leviticus 26:1; 2nd Kings 17:41, 17:12; Hosea 4:12; Jeremiah 1:16; Psalm 106:36; Revelation 9:20). Do your homework and seek Him.

The Bible says: *"For they themselves report about us what kind of a reception we had with you, and how you turned to God from idols to serve a living and true God."* *1st Thessalonians 1:9 (KJV)*

In speaking of idols, I'm going to be transparent here. For a short while, my husband and I toyed with pornography in our bedroom. It started with us being curious but before long, it became a necessity to light the fire. I can honestly say, it was no longer enjoyable to watch, and it seemed my husband and I were losing our connection to one another. I knew in my heart of hearts it just wasn't right. I felt guilt ridden. But we continued to do it anyway. We were a Christian family that prayed, studied, and served in ministry together, yet we were watching vulgar loveless acts and bringing those spirits into our existence. Heed this warning: be careful what you bring into your house!

Needless to say, God sent one of His Angels into our lives. This particular evening, we were at a ministry meeting.

After closing prayer, we were pulled aside by one of our older sisters-in-Christ. We were in the same ministry, but she really knew nothing about us other than what we presented on the surface. She began to speak a Word from God to us. Only God Himself would know the things that were coming out of her mouth. In so many words, she told us that God wanted us to clean our house of the pornography and that James, as the head, needed to make it happen. She spoke other things about not just our relationship but also my husband's childhood and his relationship with his father. Can I say #blown?

It was a defining moment in our relationship with each other and with God. I'm so thankful to God for using her as His mouthpiece, for showing us His love, grace, and mercy, for delivering us from that stronghold, and for restoring the fire in our marital bed. You talking about some goooooood nookie with hubby after that? We learned to enjoy each other again like it was the first time. When God does something, it just doesn't get any better.

When I speak of toys, they are not the traditional vibrators and other external stimuli on the market today. People get hooked on external things that I believe cross the line. Are you worshipping a false idol and not nurturing your sexual relationship with your mate? If you need to use toys for orgasm and you look forward to that outside of normal intercourse with your mate, there is a problem. The problem is with the physical, emotional, and/or spiritual connection between you and your mate. Your mate must be enough in fulfilling your needs without external stimuli. It becomes a habit. Habits are hard to break.

The toys I speak of for the purpose of enhancing your relationship are those things that will enhance the overall experience, like props. My husband and I had fuzzy cuffs for the damsel in distress; costumes for role play; feathers for tracing the body with; and the list goes on. And don't underestimate the power of wigs, which we explored already! You know, one of my favorite props ever was my husband's Timberland boots. Why? Well, mainly because it was hilarious and became one of my fondest and HOTTEST memories. Let me clue you in.

It's one of our many nights of passion. We were all over the room. In, out, here, there, upside down. We were flipping, tossing, and just having a good ol' time. The passion was mounting. He's losing traction and his feet began to slip! In the middle of this amazing nookie, he puts a pause in it and returned only to be wearing his Timbs! I'll NEVER forget that night. He needed Timbs for traction! <>

Can you think of some play things that will enhance your experience? Jot them down.

(This area intentionally left blank for notes! Think outside the box!)

- *Tasty Treats*

Having fun with delicious treats is a must if you haven't already. Think about the pu-pu platter we've already looked at. The sky is definitely the limit! When planning, though, think and prepare for any mess you may have to clean up, because the goal is to keep the mood sexy and sensual. Now, if getting messy is all a part of your plan, go with the flow and just enjoy. Have warm towels, wet naps handy, or simply bathe together as part of your playtime... that's always fun! I wouldn't come to bed toting fork, knife, and spoon. Let your hands and mouth do all the work. Finger foods tend to be easier to deal with along with food you can slurp and lick. Fruits are a perfect treat. Feed each other berries and eat them from cracks and crevices (the belly button is perfect, right?), and drizzle your favorite syrups and toppings before licking them off. Hey, why not make a sundae? Who says the pu-pu platter can't be an array of desserts? May your own rules! There are so many ways to incorporate your favorite toppings, whipped cream, fruit, syrups, and on and on 'til the break of dawn! Sharing sweet juicy fruits is always pleasant and an awesome way to initiate delectable kisses. It's light and refreshing. Try freezing fruits for a cooler experience. Create a snack ON your honey. (A little honey on your honey, perhaps?)   Build a sundae! Do you have a favorite candy? What better way to enjoy it than to eat if off the one you love? So, what are some sweet and tasty treats you can imagine using to spice up your playtime?

(This space intentionally left blank for notes)

"But the fruit of the Spirit is love, joy, peace, longsuffering, kindness, goodness, faithfulness, gentleness, self-control. Against such there is no law." Galatians 5:22

Chapter 10

The Love Nest is for Lovers

My husband and I decided early on that we would keep the kids out of our bed. We heard all those stories about how our friends barely had time for each other and if they did, they had the kids between them. I think we did the right thing. That's one battle we never had to worry about.

The first and biggest no-no in the bedroom is including the offspring! What can put a damper on the love life more than anything is having a free-for-all in the master suite. This room is your sanctuary for peace and love and a haven for lovers. I know it's difficult for some to detach from the children, but it's a must! Don't start a habit that's hard to break. The day the baby is born, think a year down the road! You don't want to have to fight every night to make your toddler stay in their own bed. Do not let your kids sleep with you.

Put this in place starting at birth. If it's a middle-of-the-night feeding, bite the bullet from day one. Get up from the bed and feed the baby from the rocking chair, after which you return the baby to his or her own bed. It'll pay off in the long run. It's important to keep your love haven a place where you can retreat to for private time without interruption. James and I had one exception: If the baby was sick with a fever, the baby would sleep with us until the fever broke, then right back to the crib or their own bedroom he went!

How do you break this habit if you've allowed your children in the bedroom? These are key:

Make the child's room inviting, enticing, pleasant, and safe. Make sure you instill a sense of pride and responsibility about their belongings in their room. Help them to make their room a haven of love, peace, security, and harmony, which includes keeping a neat and tidy room. Give them responsibilities like making the bed, opening and closing the curtains, turning the nightlight on and off daily.

Pray with your child daily and especially at bedtime that God and His angels are always present and protecting us and there is no reason to fear. Share scripture habitually and they will begin a new habit!

Be loving but firm. Understand that you created this habit that you are now having to break. Be kind. It may take some time.

Whether you start as an infant or you're breaking that habit now, understand your love life will be better off. It's easier to keep the connection with your spouse going and getting some nookie when the kids have their own space. Movie time or Saturday morning cartoon time with the kids in the love nest is a definite MAYBE, but establish the boundaries early. Think about it.

I know life happens -- the 9 to 5, your life's work, the children, and your other commitments can take up a lot of time. Do your best to create an atmosphere in your love nest to feel free, expressive, undistracted, and peaceful. What always made for a nicer experience for me was to keep things as clean and free from clutter as possible. When my boys were younger, I instituted a 15-minute family clean-up time. Four people working for 15 minutes in a concentrated area does wonders. For your bedroom, if you and your spouse took five minutes a day to tidy up, it will do wonders. I know for me clutter and things out of place are a distraction. Remove any distractions from your love nest so you can better enjoy your experience. Maybe you like to get busy on a pile of clean or dirty clothes. Hey! It's yo' thang. I'm not judging. Whatever floats your boat!

Epilogue (or something like that)

Let's Wrap it Up

"And above all things, have a fervent love for one another, for love will cover a multitude of sins." 1*st* *Peter 4:8 (NKJV)*

Well, it's time to wrap it up. The fat lady singeth. It's the end of my information sharing, and with great prayer, some marital bonding on your part and fulfilling experiences, whether it was a quickie, role playing, major foreplay involved, or one of those romps under the dining table. Your period of bonding continues, it doesn't end here. This is just a pause until the next time. A comma or semi-colon. So, what to do? Do you fall asleep in each other's arms? Cuddle? Shower together? Talk and praise your partner? Praise the Lord? Replenish your electrolytes? All of the above and more. Love unconditionally. Maintain the connectivity. Know what works for your partner and for your love life. Remember that communication is key in every aspect. Intimacy is crucial. Nurturing the relationship is critical. Love on each other like the only time you have is now. Don't wait until tomorrow to share a kiss, say I love you, send flowers, or take a walk in the park. I challenge you to do it now. Be thankful to God for your mate, your union, your experiences, and the freedom afforded you in Him.

To God be the glory for the things He has done. Peace be unto you!

"Therefore, as the elect of God, holy and beloved, put on tender mercies, kindness, humility, meekness, longsuffering; bearing with one another, and forgiving one another, if anyone has a complaint against another; even as Christ forgave you, so you also must do. But above all these things, put on love, which is the bond of perfection. And let the peace of God rule in your hearts, to which also you were called in one body; and be thankful. Let the word of Christ dwell in you richly in all wisdom, teaching and admonishing one another in psalms and hymns and spiritual songs, singing with grace in your hearts to the Lord. And whatever you do in word or deed, do all in the name of the Lord Jesus, giving thanks to God the Father through Him." Colossians 3:12-17 (NKJV)

Author's References

The Bible

The Five Love Languages, by Gary Chapman

The Act of Marriage, The Beauty of Sexual Love by Tim & Beverly LaHaye

Book Discussion Guide

1. What is the author's intention of the book? Was the intent clear? Did the author deliver?

2. Of all that was shared, do you believe there were subjects the author intentionally included and others intentionally not included?

3. What are your feelings and reactions and other readers' feelings and reactions to different challenges, scenarios, etc.?

4. What is the most important lesson you learned from reading this book?

5. Who do you think will benefit the most from this book?

6. Were any of your opinions about sex challenged after reading this book? If so, which ones?

7. How old were you when you first learned about marital sex? Who taught you? How do you think it has shaped your perception of marital sex?

8. What did your parents tell you about sex? If you have children, will you tell your children something different?

9. Was there a time when a sexual encounter or scenario didn't go as planned? Explain.

10.   How will you use this book to improve your own sex life?

Hi!

Sandy here. If you need additional copies of my book, visit www.SBSGBABIEENTERPRISES.com to purchase as well as other products and services. Don't forget to like my Facebook page, SBS Gbabie Enterprises, and follow me on Instagram, SBSGBABIEENTERPRISES, and on Twitter, @SBSGBABIE.

About the Author

Sandy Buchanan-Sumter was born and raised in the suburbs of the Nation's Capital. She's a civil servant of 30+ years and a mother of three sons, though she claims many as her own. She's a psalmist and active member of an internationally-travelled gospel group, a member of the First Baptist Church of Glenarden in Maryland, and a member of the National Congress of Black Women. Sandy is also the president and CEO of SBS GBABIE Enterprises, which focuses on helping others and providing various services. Her passion is inspiring others to be their best selves and teaching manners and etiquette to the masses. In her spare time, she loves to write, travel, cook, paint, and entertain family and friends.